W9-AHS-053

JUN - 6 2022

DEMCO

EDGE
BOOKS

The Unexplained

CROP CIRCLES

by Michael Martin

Consultant:

Benjamin Radford

Managing Editor/Investigator

Skeptical Inquirer Magazine

Amherst, New York

Capstone
press

Mankato, Minnesota

Edge Books are published by Capstone Press,
151 Good Counsel Drive, P.O. Box 669, Mankato, Minnesota 56002.
www.capstonepress.com

Library of Congress Cataloging-in-Publication Data
Martin, Michael.
  Crop circles / by Michael Martin.
    p. cm.—(Edge books. The unexplained)
  Includes bibliographical references and index.
  ISBN-13: 978-0-7368-4381-2 (hardcover)
  ISBN-10: 0-7368-4381-7 (hardcover)
  1. Crop circles. I. Title. II. Series.
AG243.M3525 2006
001.94—dc22   2005018486

Summary: Describes the history, sightings, and search for the causes of
    crop circles.

Editorial Credits

Katy Kudela, editor; Juliette Peters, set designer; Kate Opseth and Thomas Emery, book
    designers; Kelly Garvin, photo researcher/photo editor

Photo Credits

Corbis/Ian Rose; Frank Lane Picture Agency, 27 (right); Paul Chinn/San Francisco
    Chronicle, 23
Fortean Picture Library, 7, 11, 25, 29; Frederick C. Taylor, cover, 9, 10, 14, 15; Philippa
    Foster, 5, 18, 26; Robert Irving, 13; Shin-ichiro Namiki, 17, 19
Mary Evans Picture Library, 27 (left); Stacy Collection, 21

1 2 3 4 5 6 11 10 09 08 07 06

TABLE OF CONTENTS

FEATURES

Chapter 1

MYSTERIES IN THE FIELDS

One summer night in 1999, a young man in the Netherlands saw something unusual. He claimed it was a small light above the field behind his house. The man thought the light might be a star. But the faint pink light began to move. It floated above the field and seemed to shine down on one section of the field. Then the light slowly faded and disappeared.

The young man ran into the field to investigate. He found the crops swirled into a circular pattern. The crops and soil were still warm. He had discovered a crop circle.

Learn about:
• Netherlands mystery
• Crop circle sightings
• A worldwide mystery

Bright lights are sometimes linked with crop circles. People claim they have seen strange lights near crop circle fields.

Strange Appearances

Crop circles are mysterious patterns that appear in farm fields. They form most often during summer nights. Almost all crop circles appear in wheat, barley, or oat fields. The fields usually show no footprints or other signs of entry. The plant stalks are bent but not broken.

It is a rare event to see a crop circle as it forms. But at least 80 people say they have witnessed the event. Some witnesses say they have seen strange lights near where the circles appear in the crops.

Crop circles appear in fields around the world. People have reported crop circles in at least 28 countries. Southern England has the highest number of reported crop circles.

In 2001, people found a huge crop circle in England. The formation was 900 feet (274 meters) wide. The crop circle had a pattern of 409 small circles.

▲ A crop circle's pattern can have many circles like this crop circle in southern England.

Chapter 2

HISTORY OF CROP CIRCLES

Some people claim crop circles have occurred for hundreds of years. But researchers say crop circles didn't appear until the 1970s. The first few crop circles mysteriously appeared in the United States and England. By the 1980s, hundreds of crop circles had shown up in southern England. These large crop circles caught the world's attention.

Different Designs

The early English crop circles had fairly simple designs. They were plain circles or circles surrounded by rings. Sometimes the circles had a cross inside.

Learn about:
- England's crop circles
- An early legend
- Crop circles made by humans

England's crop circles amazed the world.
These circles appeared in 1988.

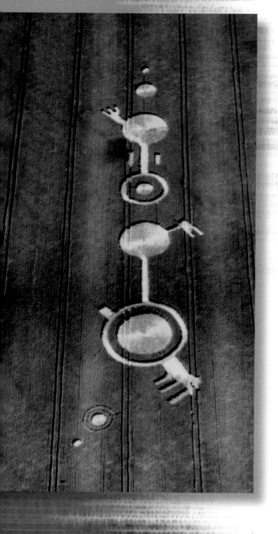

During the late 1980s, new designs began to appear. The designs were a mixture of straight lines and symbols.

In 1990, crop circles in England became larger and full of details. Some circles included ancient designs and religious symbols. The shape of a Jewish holy candleholder called a menorah appeared in a field. One crop circle even showed a map of the earth's solar system.

A Crop Circle Legend

Some people believe crop circles first appeared in the 1600s. One famous report is from the summer of 1678 in England.

Legend holds a farmer became angry with his hired helper. The two men could not agree on payment for cutting the field. The farmer claimed he would rather pay the devil himself to cut the field. Late that night, a light appeared in the farmer's field. The next morning, the crops were cut in circles.

Researchers do not believe this legend is proof of an ancient crop circle. They point out that the legend says the crops were cut down. But plants in crop circle fields are bent.

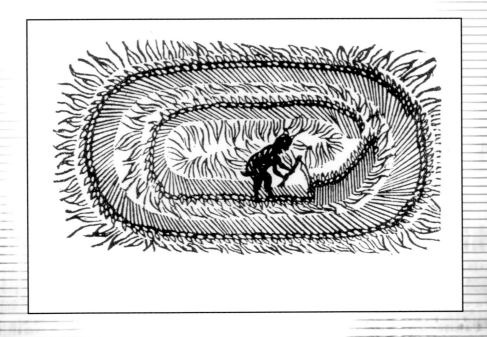

Pranks with Planks

In 1991, the story of two Englishmen made news headlines. Doug Bower and Dave Chorley claimed they created crop circles in England. They said they used planks and rope to make the circles. Over a 13-year period, the men claimed they formed 250 crop circles. They said they made the crop circles as a hoax.

Many people believed the story of the Englishmen. But other people still had doubts. They did not think the two men had the strength or the time to make so many crop circles by themselves. They also thought it was strange that no one ever reported seeing the men making the crop circles.

EDGE FACT

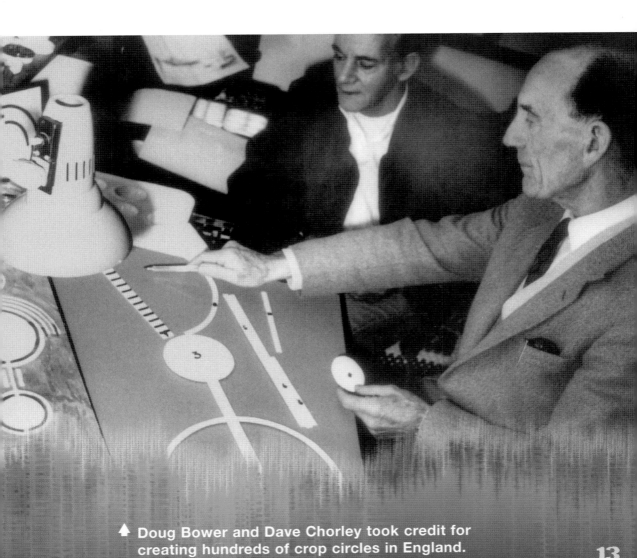

▲ Doug Bower and Dave Chorley took credit for creating hundreds of crop circles in England.

Testing the Claims

A group of researchers decided to test the claim of the Englishmen. They used wooden planks and rope to create their own crop circles. Their studies showed that crop circles could be made by humans.

The researchers also may have solved another crop circle mystery. Most crop circles show no footsteps or other signs of entry. But the researchers found they could easily walk on tracks left by tractors. The soil on the tracks was too hard and dry to leave footprints.

Simple tools might be the answer to how people can make crop circles.

With time, patience, and a few tools, researchers have shown that people can create crop circles.

Chapter 3

SEARCHING THE FIELDS

After many years of research, scientists agreed that people did make some crop circles. But did they make all of them? The search for proof sent plant scientists and researchers into the fields to find out.

Plant Life Inside Crop Circles

Some plant scientists have studied the plants found inside crop circles. They found evidence that showed the plants were once under intense heat. But intense heat lasting longer than a few seconds would have started the plants on fire.

Learn about:
• Finding mixed answers
• Cereologists
• Strange stories

People study flattened crops in crop circles hoping to find answers.

A few plant scientists reported that a strange brown glaze covered plants in crop circles. This finding, along with the heated plant stalks, was a puzzle. The mystery led some scientists to believe that not all crop circles were hoaxes.

▼ Some people believe whirlwinds of air create crop circles.

A Natural Cause

Dr. Terence Meaden, member of the Tornado and Storm Research Organization in England, was one of the first scientists to study crop circles. He thought crop circles had a natural cause. He believed that small currents of swirling winds could flatten the crops into circles. Whirlwinds are often found in hilly areas, such as southern England.

The number of crop circle reports is quickly growing. People report about 250 new sightings each year.

▲ People believe a natural cause such as wind could bend plants without breaking them.

Cereologists in the Fields

Plant scientists are just one group of people looking for answers. People who study crop circles are called cereologists. Cereologists are often the first researchers to visit a crop circle field. They measure and photograph crop circles. They then study the photographs to figure out how the patterns were made. They also look to see if the patterns are a symbol.

Cereologists look for clues inside and outside of the crop circle. They meet with people living near the crop circle sites. They never know what they are going to find. Some cereologists have heard strange stories of animals reacting to crop circles. Farmers have claimed that their horses and sheep refuse to go near crop circle fields. Other farmers recall their animals acting strangely a few hours before a crop circle appeared.

▲ Cereologists step carefully when they are walking around in a crop circle. They do not want to destroy any clues.

Other Odd Happenings

Some people report unusual feelings while entering a crop circle. They suddenly feel sick or uncomfortable. Once outside the circle, they feel well again. At other times, people report a great sense of well-being inside a crop circle.

Other people claim everyday objects show hints of unseen forces in crop circles. Visitors have reported that their watches and cameras stopped working inside crop circles. But not everyone has had this experience. Many people have taken photographs inside crop circles. There is no strong research to show that crop circles are responsible for watches and cameras failing to work.

On July 11, 1991, a huge crop circle appeared near England's Barbury Castle. Local residents remember seeing strange lights. They also heard a loud noise that sounded like thunder.

▲ Some people claim crop circles make them feel happy and content.

Chapter 4

LOOKING FOR ANSWERS

Over the years, crop circle designs have grown more detailed. In 2000, a huge crop circle appeared in Woodborough Hill, England. The crop circle had 308 triangles around it. Some people do not believe humans made these patterns. They think aliens created this detailed crop circle.

How or why would aliens be making crop circles on earth? Some people believe alien spacecraft leave markings when they land on earth. Other people believe crop circles are secret messages from aliens to humans.

Learn about:
- Alien messages
- Ball lightning
- An English legend

Crop circles have turned farm fields into art. In 2002, this crop circle appeared in southern England.

Trying to Solve the Mystery

Some people think that the strange lights seen near crop circles are a clue. They think lights might be signs of alien spacecrafts. But most unidentified flying object (UFO) sightings are not associated with crop circles.

Skeptical people believe events in nature can explain the source of crop circles. Some people wonder if crop circles are made by a natural energy, such as ball lightning. This ball of light suddenly appears and then vanishes. Other people agree with Dr. Meaden's theory. They think wind forces can create patterns in farm fields.

▼ Bright lights sometimes appear in a field before a crop circle forms.

Fairy Rings

Farm fields aren't the only places plagued with strange circles. During the spring and summer, circles also appear in some lawns. These circles are dark green or brown. They range from a few inches or centimeters to 50 feet (15 meters) wide. Sometimes mushrooms appear on the outer edges.

What causes these mysterious circles? Hundreds of years ago, people thought these circles were signs of the devil and witches. In England, people called these circles fairy rings. Legend says fairies held dances late at night. They made a ring and used the mushrooms to rest on between dances.

Today, scientists know these rings have a natural cause. A fungus in the ground forms the rings.

Folk art shows the legend of fairy dances.

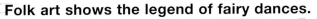

Fairy rings

EDGE FACT

Colin Andrews, a cereologist, believes about 80 percent of crop circles are made by humans. He says that the other 20 percent are probably the work of an unknown force.

Still a Mystery

The mystery behind crop circles has not been solved. Scientists and researchers agree that many, if not most, crop circles are probably made by humans. If crop circles are made by strange winds, aliens, or mysterious forces, more research is needed to prove these theories. But as long as crop circles continue to appear, people will be drawn to the mystery.

▲ Although crop circles take on familiar shapes, people are still unsure if all crop circles are made by humans.

GLOSSARY

alien (AY-lee-uhn)—a creature from another planet

ball lightning (BAWL LITE-ning)—a type of lightning that can float in the air; some people think ball lightning can create crop circles.

cereologist (SIHR-ee-ohl-uh-jist)—a person who studies crop circles

fungus (FUHN-guhss)—a type of plant that has no leaves, flowers, or roots; mushrooms and molds are fungi.

hoax (HOHKS)—a trick to make people believe something that is not true

legend (LEJ-uhnd)—a story handed down from earlier times; legends are stories that are not always true.

READ MORE

Burns, Jan. *Crop Circles.* Wonders of the World. San Diego: KidHaven Press, 2005.

Mason, Paul. *UFO's and Crop Circles.* Marvels and Mysteries. North Mankato, Minn.: Smart Apple Media, 2005.

Oxlade, Chris. *The Mystery of Crop Circles.* Can Science Solve? Des Plaines, Ill.: Heinemann Library, 2001.

INTERNET SITES

FactHound offers a safe, fun way to find Internet sites related to this book. All of the sites on FactHound have been researched by our staff.

Here's how:
1. Visit *www.facthound.com*
2. Type in this special code **0736843817** for age-appropriate sites. Or enter a search word related to this book for a more general search.
3. Click on the **Fetch It** button.

FactHound will fetch the best sites for you!

INDEX